OTHER BOOKS BY JEFF SMITH

THE FIRST TRILOGY

BONE VOLUME ONE: OUT FROM BONEVILLE

BONE VOLUME TWO: THE GREAT COW RACE

BONE VOLUME THREE: EYES OF THE STORM

THE SECOND TRILOGY

BONE VOLUME FOUR: THE DRAGONSLAYER

BONE VOLUME FIVE: ROCKJAW, MASTER OF THE EASTERN BORDER

BONE VOLUME SIX: OLD MAN'S CAVE

(COMING SOON)
BONE VOLUME SEVEN: GHOST CIRCLES

OLD MAN'S CAVE

Volume Six:
Old Man's Cave

Jeff Smith

Cartoon Books
Columbus, Ohio

THIS BOOK IS
FOR
JIM KAMMERUD

BONE Volume Six: Old Man's Cave copyright ® 1999 by Jeff Smith
All rights reserved. No part of this book may be reproduced or utilized in any form or by any means, electronic or mechanical, includ-
ing photocopying, recording, or by any information storage or retrieval system, without written permission except in the case of reprints
in the context of reviews. The chapters in this book were originally published in the comic book BONE and are copyright © 1998 and
1999 by Jeff Smith. BONE® is © 1999 Jeff Smith. Acknowledgements: The Harvestar Family Crest designed by Charles Vess.
Artwork on cover by: Jeff Smith and Elizabeth Lewis.
For information write:
Cartoon Books
P.O. Box 16973
Columbus, OH 43216

Hardcover ISBN: 1-888963-04-2
Softcover ISBN: 1-888963-05-0
Library of Congress Catalog Card Number: 95-68403

10 9 8 7 6 5 4 3 2

Printed in Canada

After being run out of Boneville, the three bone cousins, Fone Bone, Phoney Bone, and Smiley Bone, are separated and lost in a vast uncharted desert.

One by one, they find their way into a deep, forested valley filled with wonderful and terrifying creatures . . .

LAST I SAW THORN SHE WAS RESCUING THE GREAT RED DRAGON FROM PHONEY BONE'S **LYNCH MOB.**

OH NO!

I KNEW IT! I KNEW IT HAD SOMETHING TO DO WITH PHONEY! **WHAT HAPPENED?**

THORN **SAVED THE DRAGON,** BUT AT THAT VERY **SAME MOMENT,** THE RAT CREATURES **INVADED** THE VALLEY!

THAT'S TH' **SMOKE** YOU SAW! THOSE MONSTERS ARE BURNING EVERY FARM IN THEIR **PATH!**

OHMYGOSH.

LUCKILY, AIN'T NOBODY BEEN **KILT** YET, AS FAR AS I **KNOWS,** BUT LOTSA FOLKS IS **HOMELESS** AN' **SCARED!**

WAIT'LL I GET MY HANDS ON THAT **NO-GOOD, SELFISH COUSIN** OF OURS -- HIM AND THAT **STUPID STAR SHIRT** HE ALWAYS WEARS!

EVER SINCE WE **CAME** TO THIS VALLEY THE RAT CREATURES HAVE BEEN SEARCHING FOR *THE ONE WHO BEARS THE STAR* --

-- BECAUSE **THEY** THINK PHONEY'S A THREAT TO THEM, AN' NOW THEY'RE SEARCHING FOR **US** BECAUSE THEY THINK WE KILLED **KINGDOK!**

YOU KNOW WHAT THE **WORST** THING IS? BECAUSE OF **US,** THE ENEMY KNOWS **THORN** IS A MEMBER OF THE LOST ROYAL FAMILY. NOW **SHE'S** IN DANGER, TOO.

MAYBE THAT GROUND HOG WAS RIGHT. WE **ARE** TROUBLE!

WELL, C'MON, TED, TAKE US **BACK.**

LET'S GET TO THE BOTTOM OF THIS *"ONE WHO BEARS THE STAR"* BUSINESS BEFORE SOMEONE REALLY **DOES** GET HURT --

OR **WORSE!**

RUMORS ARE RUNNING WILD UP AND DOWN THE FRONT LINES THAT **KINGDOK IS DEAD!**

?!!

Shoss! NESSEN! NESSEN!

IK GAREN SPEK NESSEN!

WHAT ARE THEY SAYING? I DON'T UNDERSTAND.

Shh!

WELL, **I** UNDERSTOOD 'EM **PLENTY!** THEY'RE LOOKIN' FOR A **BALD CREATURE** WHO BEARS A **STAR!** SOUND LIKE ANYBODY YOU KNOW?!

WENDELL! KEEP QUIET!

I KNEW YOU WERE NO GOOD, BONE! I SHOULDA LISTENED TO **LUCIUS!** JUST WAIT'LL WE GET BACK TO TOWN, YOU RUNT, I'LL FIX YOU **GOOD!**

THEY ARE TURNING AROUND. HEADING BACK **EAST!**

WHAT TH' HECK WAS **THAT** ALL ABOUT? THEY SEEMED PRETTY **UPSET** ABOUT SOMETHING!

THEY'RE IN A STATE OF **CONFUSION--**

THERE ARE RUMORS THEIR CHIEFTAIN HAS BEEN **KILLED.**

ALL THE PATROL TEAMS ARE RETURNING TO THEIR BASE CAMPS TO FIND OUT WHAT IS GOING ON.

HOW CAN YOU TELL **THAT**? THEY WERE TALKING IN SOME KIND OF **JIBBERISH!**

THEY WERE SPEAKING **NESSEN** . . . AN ANCIENT RAT CREATURE LANGUAGE RESERVED FOR TIMES OF WAR AND MILITARY EMERGENCY.

OH, REALLY? AND WHEN DID YOU LEARN TO SPEAK AN ANCIENT RAT CREATURE **MILITARY LANGUAGE?!**

I **DIDN'T.** BUT FOR SOME REASON I UNDERSTOOD EVERY SINGLE WORD THEY SAID.

MRS. TANNER, WE HAVE SOME FOOD AND WATER FOR YOUR FAMILY AT A SMALL CAMP NOT FAR FROM HERE...

...THAT'S WHERE THE REST OF THE VILLAGERS ARE. WE'RE GOING TO SEND YOU BACK THERE UNTIL WE CAN DETERMINE THAT THE TOWN IS SAFE.

WHY IS THIS HAPPENING, THORN? WHY ARE THE HAIRY MEN DOING THIS?

WE'RE TRYING TO FIND OUT.

I THINK WE KNOW ENOUGH! LET'S STRING THE LITTLE RUNT UP RIGHT NOW!

NO. WE'RE GOING TO THE TOWN. IT'S A CLOUDLESS NIGHT, SO WE'LL KEEP TO THE RAVINES. SAM CAN TAKE THE TANNERS BACK TO OUR CAMP. JON, WENDELL AND EUCLID, YOU KNOW THE ROUTINE. LET'S GO.

I SWEAR I DON'T KNOW WHAT THE RAT CREATURES WANT, THORN! THIS IS ALL SOME KINDA CRAZY MIX UP!

THEY'RE NOT JUST AFTER ME, THEY'RE AFTER SOME PRINCESS! I'M INNOCENT, THORN! YA GOTTA BELIEVE ME!

I DO BELIEVE YOU. THAT'S THE ONLY REASON I HAVEN'T LET WENDELL AND EUCLID STRING YOU UP.

YOU-- YOU MEAN IT? YOU BELIEVE ME?

YES, I DO. WOULD YOU BELIEVE ME IF I SAID THE PRINCESS WAS INNOCENT, TOO?

!

NOW LET'S GO SEE WHAT'S LEFT OF OUR TOWN.

OH, NO...

NO...

THIS CAN'T BE RIGHT. WE MUST'VE TAKEN A WRONG TURN.

I'M **SURE** THIS IS IT... BUT... BUT...

IT'S **GONE!** THE ENTIRE VILLAGE IS **GONE!**

IT CAN'T BE... THERE'S NOTHING LEFT...

THEY COULDN'T HAVE DESTROYED OUR **WHOLE TOWN** - -

WHERE'S THE **BARRELHAVEN** TAVERN?

WE'RE STANDING IN IT.

STOP ACTING LIKE AN **ANIMAL**. HASN'T THERE BEEN ENOUGH VIOLENCE? NOW PUT PHONEY BONE **DOWN**.

NO!! HE SWINDLED US AND **DESTROYED** OUR TOWN!

HE DIDN'T ATTACK THE VILLAGE! THE **RAT CREATURES** DID!

HE TRICKED US INTO CHASIN' AFTER **DRAGONS!** WE WERE AWAY FROM OUR **HOMES** WHEN WE SHOULDA BEEN **HERE** DEFENDING THE **VILLAGE!**

NOBODY **FORCED** YOU TO FOLLOW HIM! YOU WERE A **MOB** LOOKING FOR SCAPEGOATS!

BUT IF WE HAD BEEN **HERE**, THEN LUCIUS MIGHT STILL BE **ALIVE!**

WE DON'T KNOW WHAT HAPPENED TO LUCIUS. . . BUT WHATEVER IT WAS, IF YOU **HAD** BEEN HERE, YOU WOULD HAVE **SHARED** HIS FATE!

AND SO WOULD ALL THE OTHER VILLAGERS WHO WERE **WITH** YOU HUNTING DRAGONS! THIS BONE PROBABLY SAVED **HALF THE VILLAGE** BY TAKING YOU UP INTO THE MOUNTAINS!

WHY ARE YOU DEFENDING HIM? **YOU** HEARD THE HAIRY MEN -- THEY'RE SEARCHING TH' WHOLE **VALLEY** FOR THE ONE WHO **BEARS THE STAR!**

AND A **PRINCESS!** THEY'RE LOOKING FOR A **PRINCESS**, TOO! **RIGHT, THORN?**

SHUT UP, YOU!

SCRNCH

GURK!

KEEP IT UP, EUCLID! THE MORE WE BEHAVE LIKE **BRUTES**, THE MORE POWER OUR **ENEMIES** HAVE!

WHAT DO **YOU** SAY, WENDELL? DO WE **STRING HIM UP** OR **NOT**?

I DON'T KNOW...

GIK GURK

I NEVER IMAGINED THIS

MAYBE THORN'S **RIGHT**. THERE'S BEEN **ENOUGH** VIOLENCE.

YOU DON'T WANNA LET HIM **OFF THE HOOK**, DO YA?

GERK!

WE'RE AS MUCH TO BLAME AS HE IS! GET A **HOLD OF YOURSELF!**

I'LL GET HOLD OF MYSELF RIGHT AFTER I **TWIST HIS SCRAWNY NECK!**

IT'S THORN!! IT'S **THORN!** SHE'S TH' **PRINCESS!**

GO ON, YER MAJESTY, ORDER THIS APE OFF OF ME!

PRINCESS? LIKE A **PRINCESS** PRINCESS?

YEAH, THAT'S **RIGHT!** AN' THAT MEANS GRAN'MA BEN IS HER **FAIRY GODMOTHER,** SO YOU'RE IN **BIG TROUBLE,** BUDDY!

DON'T HELP ME, PHONEY!

THE RAT CREATURES **WERE SEARCHING FOR A PRINCESS...**

OKAY, OKAY, THE RAT CREATURES **MAY** THINK I'M A PRINCESS, **THAT** MUCH IS TRUE.

A **PRINCESS**? **HOW**? FROM **WHERE**?! THE ROYAL FAMILY WAS KILLED IN THE BIG WAR!

THERE HASN'T BEEN A KINGDOM FOR ALMOST FIFTEEN YEARS!

YES, I KNOW THAT. **EVERYBODY** KNOWS THAT --EXCEPT, APPARENTLY, FOR THE **RAT CREATURES** AND MY **GRAN'MA BEN**. THEY DEFINITELY THINK I'M A PRINCESS.

BUT THAT DOESN'T MEAN I **AM** A PRINCESS NECESSARILY--

SHE DOES KINDA **LOOK** LIKE A PRINCESS.

YES, BUT WHAT DOES THAT MAKE OL' **ROSE BEN**? THE LOST QUEEN OF THE **VALLEY**? OL' GRAN'MA BEN RACES **COWS**, REMEMBER. . .

LOOK, I DON'T KNOW IF IT'S TRUE. . . BUT I AM SURE WE SHOULDN'T BE DISCUSSING IT **HERE**!

THAT MEANS **YOU** CAN JUST KEEP YOUR **TRAP SHUT** -- UNDERSTAND?

YEAH, YEAH. WE ALL GOT OUR LITTLE **DELUSIONS OF GRANDEUR**. I COULD TELL YOU WANTED TO GET IT OFF YOUR CHEST.

LISTEN UP. THIS WAR CLUB BELONGS TO MY FRIEND **FONE BONE**. I FOUND IT HERE IN THE WRECKAGE OF THE BARN, AND THERE'S A GOOD CHANCE HE AND SOME OTHERS ESCAPED. . .

... I FOUND SOME **TRACKS** LEADING AWAY FROM THE COMPOUND INTO THE WOODS. **I WANT TO FOLLOW THEIR TRAIL.**

FORGET THAT! AS FAR AS **I'M** CONCERNED, TH' **BONES** KILLED **LUCIUS!**

HEY! YOU CAN BLAME **ME** ALL YOU WANT, **PAL,** BUT WATCH YER **MOUTH** WHEN YOU'RE TALKIN' ABOUT MY **COUSINS!**

I'LL GO **ALONE,** IF I HAVE TO.

GRR!

GRR!

BUT THORN, WE HAVE A CAMP FULL OF HURT AND FRIGHTENED PEOPLE BACK THERE. ARE YOU JUST GOING TO ABANDON **THEM?**

I CAN'T ABANDON MY **FRIEND!**

THORN! MISS THORN!

LOOK WHAT **I** FOUND! IT'S A **NOTE** TO **FONE BONE!**

THAT'S **MY** NOTE! WHERE DID YOU FIND IT?

IN THE HOLLOW TREE THAT LUCIUS AN' I USE TO PASS **MESSAGES** TO EACH OTHER.

HMM. **THAT'S** STRANGE. HOW DID IT GET THERE?

WHAT'S IT SAY?

"I HAVE GONE HOME TO GRAN'MA'S FARM."

I WROTE THIS THE NIGHT I LEFT THE COMPOUND SO FONE BONE WOULD KNOW WHERE I WENT...

Dear Fone Bone, I have gone home to Gran'ma's farm. Please don't worry -- just need to sort things out. If you leave the valley before we see other 'bye.

LUCIUS MUST'VE **FOUND** THE NOTE.

AND HE PUT IT IN THE TREE FOR **YOU** TO FIND, JON.

WHY?

SNIFF.

WAIT! I KNOW!

BECAUSE **HE** WENT TO GRAN'MA BEN'S FARM TO LOOK FOR **THORN!**

BLOODY STARS!!

IF HE'S **RIGHT,** THEN LUCIUS MIGHT STILL BE **ALIVE!**

YEAH! MAYBE **ALL** OUR NEIGHBORS ARE STILL ALIVE!

FIRST THING IN THE MORNING, WE HEAD NORTH TO GRAN'MA BEN'S PLACE.

RIGHT!

YOU GO.

I HAVE TO LOOK FOR FONE BONE. WILL YOU BE COMING WITH ME, PHONCIBLE?

WHO **ME?** YOU MEAN OUT **THERE?!**

GULP. EEH. YEAH... I'LL GO...

WELL, AT LEAST YOU'RE NOT A **COWARD!**

OR ARE YOU **MORE** AFRAID TO BE LEFT WITH **THEM?**

ME? AFRAID?! **YEAH, RIGHT!** YOU'RE GONNA **NEED** A GUY WITH MY SKILLS FOR **PROTECTION!**

HMM. ON SECOND THOUGHT, IT **WILL** BE DANGEROUS. MAYBE I SHOULD GO ALONE.

YOU AREN'T **INVINCIBLE**, YOU KNOW. WHAT DO YOU WANT ME TO TELL YOUR GRAN'MA IF YOU GET HURT?

DON'T WORRY, WENDELL, I CAN TAKE CARE OF MYSELF.

FAMOUS LAST WORDS. . .

WHOA!

TURN AROUND QUICK! WE GOT COMPANY!

STICK-EATERS!

UM . . .
I THINK THIS MIGHT BE
FOR ME.

HELLO?

CAN I
HELP YOU?

WE BRING A
MESSAGE
TO YOU
FROM YOUR
GRANDMOTHER.

SHE IS
WAITING FOR
YOU AT **OLD
MAN'S CAVE.**

SHE BIDS
YOU TO
JOIN HER
IMMEDIATELY.

OLD MAN'S CAVE...

HOW DO I KNOW I CAN TRUST YOU?

BEFORE I CAN GO TO OLD MAN'S CAVE, I MUST FIND MY FRIEND **FONE BONE.**

YOUR GRANDMOTHER BIDS YOU TO JOIN HER **IMMEDIATELY.**

HELP ME FIND MY FRIEND **FIRST.**

YOU **HAVE** TO HELP ME, DON'T YOU? IT IS YOUR **DUTY.**

WE ARE BUT GUIDES.

YOU ALONE MAY WALK YOUR PATH.

THEN GUIDE ME. SHOULD I SEARCH FOR MY **FRIEND?** OR SHOULD I GO TO **OLD MAN'S CAVE?**

YOUR FRIEND WAS LAST SEEN **FAR AWAY** IN THE EASTERN MOUNTAINS. HE IS RUMORED TO HAVE BEEN INVOLVED IN THE DEATH OF THE MIGHTY **KINGDOK,** AND MANY ARMIES ARE NOW **SEARCHING** FOR HIM...

OH, MY!

BUT REMEMBER... YOU HAVE A **GREATER** DUTY TO YOUR PEOPLE.

CHOOSE, YOUNG ONE. TIME IS SHORT.

WHAT DO I DO?

I HAVE NO IDEA.

FONE BONE WOULD KNOW.

YOUR **MAJESTY,** OLD MAN'S CAVE IS ON THE WAY TO YOUR GRANDMOTHER'S **FARM!** WE SHOULD GO THERE! PERHAPS LUCIUS AND THE OTHERS ARE ALREADY THERE **WAITING** FOR US!

I DON'T KNOW. IT'S SO HARD TO THINK. I'LL DECIDE IN THE MORNING.

YOU HEARD THE **PRINCESS!** WE'RE STOPPING FOR THE NIGHT! **JON,** YOU HAVE THE FIRST WATCH!

YES, SIR!

NEXT: SOUP FOR THE SOUL

THORN COULD'VE FOUND HER WAY THROUGH THIS RAIN. **SHE COULD FIND HER WAY IN TH' DARKEST NIGHT** LIKE SHE WAS FOLLOWING A MAP.

YES, SHE COULD. IT'S **UNCANNY.**

hmmf.

SHE FOLLOWS THE **DRAGONS IN THE EARTH.** JUST LIKE TH' DRAGON TOLD HER.

YEAH, WELL, SHE'S FOLLOWIN' DRAGONS **SOMEWHERE ELSE! FORGET HER!** WE GOT PROBLEMS OF OUR OWN--

HEY!

THAT'S IT-- I'VE **HAD IT!**

SPLOSH!

EUCLID! SAVE IT FOR LATER! THERE COULD BE RAT CREATURES **TWENTY FEET AWAY** FOR ALL WE KNOW!

WHERE'S YER **LITTLE PRINCESS,** NOW? HUH, BONE? SHE'S NOT HERE TO SAVE YA!

PUT HIM **DOWN,** EUCLID!

STAY BACK! I'VE HAD IT WITH THIS **TROUBLEMAKER!** THIS IS ALL HIS **FAULT!**

ALL RIGHT, THAT'S ENOUGH. I DON'T KNOW WHERE THORN **IS,** BUT UNTIL SHE GETS BACK, I'M **ENFORCING HER ORDERS!**

YOU'RE A **FOOL,** WENDELL! SHE RAN OUT ON US LAST NIGHT! WHAT DO YOU **CARE** WHAT SHE WANTS?!

I'M F-FREEZING, FONE BONE... CAN'T WE STOP FOR A **MINUTE**?

WE GOTTA KEEP **MOVIN'**, SMILEY.

TRY TO KEEP YOUR MIND ON OTHER THINGS!

BUT I'M GETTIN' SO SLEEPY...

PINCH YOURSELF --

WE HAVE TO GET BACK! I'M WORRIED THAT SOMETHING **BAD** HAS HAPPENED!

THAT WAY. OLD MAN'S CAVE IS DIRECTLY THAT WAY.

WOW! WE WERE HEADING IN TH' WRONG DIRECTION!

GREAT! LET'S GET GOIN'! GRAN'MA'S AWAITIN' ON US!

HEY, THORN! YOU'RE GOING THE WRONG WAY! YOU JUST SAID OLD MAN'S CAVE IS **THIS** WAY!

WE'RE NOT GOING TO OLD MAN'S CAVE. THERE'S NOBODY THERE WE CAN **TRUST.**

NOW, C'MON. WE NEED TO FIND SHELTER.

IF YOU COULD SEE THE OMEN THAT ANNOUNCED THEIR COMING...

...YOU TOO WOULD BELIEVE THEM TO BE POWERFUL ENOUGH TO **FREE** YOU FROM YOUR PRISION OF STONE...

WE BEGIN TO LOSE OUR PATIENCE...

IF YOU TRULY WISHED TO FREE US...

YOU WOULD HAVE BROUGHT THE PRINCESS BEFORE US...

MANY ATTEMPTS HAVE BEEN MADE TO REACH THE **VENI-YAN-CARI**... BUT SHE HAS AWAKENED AND REPELS OUR CALLS...

OFTEN SHE REPELS US WITH THE HELP OF THE **BONES**...

AGAIN, IT WAS THE **BONE CREATURES** WHO LED US TO **DISCOVER** THAT THE PRINCESS WAS STILL **ALIVE** - -

SILENCE!

ENOUGH ABOUT THIS STAR BEARER!

MASTER...
PLEASE DO NOT BE ANGRY...
OUR PLAN IS **WORKING!**

OUR MILITARY OBJECTIVE... TO CAUSE WIDESPREAD FEAR AND PANIC HAS BEEN ACCOMPLISHED... WE HAVE SWEPT ACROSS THE VALLEY AND BACK... DESTROYING EVERY FARM IN OUR PATH...

THE FLAT-LANDERS ARE BECOMING DISCONNECTED... THE STAR BEARER HAS **HELPED** BY SEWING SEEDS OF DISTRUST AGAINST THE DRAGONS!

REACH OUT!
DO YOU NOT **FEEL IT?**
THE **BARRIER** IS BREAKING UP!
SOON YOU WILL BE **FREE...**

YES... IT IS TRUE... WE ARE COMING CLOSER TO THE SURFACE...

THEN HEAR ME, O LORD... THE PRINCESS SURELY HAS THE POWER TO **FREE** YOU... BUT SHE ALSO HAS THE STRENGTH TO **DESTROY YOU --**

... PERHAPS YOU ARE JEALOUS OF THE PRINCESS AND THAT IS WHY YOU PREFER THE STAR BEARER...

MASTER... I AM BUT YOUR HUMBLE SERVANT... I MERELY PROPOSE THAT THE VENI-YAN-CARI IS MORE POWERFUL AND POSES A GREATER **RISK** SHOULD IT BECOME NECESSARY TO PREFORM A **SACRIFICE...**

AND SHE WOULD TAKE YOUR PLACE AS OUR EYES AND HANDS...

PLEASE... MY LORD, IF YOU COULD SEE THE **OMEN...** YOU WOULD KNOW THAT THE ONE WHO BEARS THE STAR... WHILE NOT AS POWERFUL AS THE VENI-YAN-CARI... ... WILL BE STRONG ENOUGH ... AND WITH LESS RISK TO YOURSELF.

YES... YOU ARE RIGHT...

YES...

FOR NOW AT LEAST... YOU ARE OUR EYES...

IF THIS OMEN THAT ANNOUNCED THE ONE WHO BEARS THE STAR IS AS POWERFUL AS YOU SAY... THEN YOU MAY CONTINUE YOUR SEARCH FOR THIS CREATURE...

...BUT IF YOU ARE WRONG...

...THEN BE PREPARED FOR YOUR END TO BE VERY... ...VERY... PAINFUL...

NEXT: UNHOLY ALLIANCES....

I'M NOT SURE I **DO!** IF ANYBODY WANTS **MY** ADVICE, AN' CLEARLY NO ONE **DOES**, I SAY WE NEED TO GET TO **OLD MAN'S CAVE!**

HE'S **RIGHT**, THORN. WE CAN'T DO THIS ALONE. GRAN'MA BEN AND ALL THE VILLAGERS ARE **THERE**.

I TOLD YOU, FONE BONE, WE'RE NOT GOING TO OLD MAN'S CAVE. THERE'S NO ONE THERE WE CAN **TRUST**.

YOU CAN TRUST **GRAN'MA BEN!**

I SAID NO. NOW, PLEASE GO BACK ON PATROL, AND MAKE SURE THAT ANYONE WHO COMES THIS WAY-- ANY BIRD, ANY ANIMAL, OR ANY INSECT-- **ANYONE** -- IS TURNED AWAY WITHOUT SEEING US.

ALL RIGHT, I'M **GOIN'.** BUT WHEN THIS IS ALL OVER, GRAN'MA BEN GONNA SQUISH ME LIKE A **BUG** FOR DISOBEYIN' HER.

ARE YOU **SURE** ABOUT GRAN'MA BEN? 'CAUSE TO TELL TH' **TRUTH**, I KINDA **MISS** HER.

EXCUSE ME. . . I'M GOING TO FIX SOME SUPPER. WOULD YOU MIND HANDING ME SOME OF THAT FUEL, SMILEY?

YEAH, OKAY. . .

IT'S JUST THAT MAYBE I DON'T UNDERSTAND TH' **PLAN**.

COULD YOU MAKE A LITTLE PILE WITH THOSE DROPPINGS?

DROPPINGS? EEYUU!

DRIED ANIMAL DROPPINGS.

MAKES A SMOKELESS FIRE.

WE CAN WORK ON OUR PLAN WHILE WE EAT.

THORN, WE DON'T **HAVE** A PLAN.

YEAH, HOW ARE WE GONNA **GET** THE HOODED ONE? WE DON'T KNOW NOTHIN' **ABOUT** HIM EXCEPT THAT HE APPEARS IN YOUR **DREAMS.**

WE KNOW HE HAS AN **ARMY** THAT'S OUT HUNTING FOR YOU AND OUR COUSIN PHONEY BONE.

YEAH, THORN, WHO **IS** THIS GUY, ANYWAY?

I DON'T KNOW. THERE'S A PROTECTIVE SPELL AROUND THE HOODED ONE SIMILAR TO THE ONE TED AND I PUT AROUND THE FOUR OF **US.**

. . . BUT I DO KNOW **SOME** THINGS.

I KNOW THE HOODED ONE DRAWS HIS POWER FROM A DREAM BEING CALLED THE **LORD OF THE LOCUSTS.**

THESE POWERS LET THE HOODED ONE TRAVEL IN - -AND IN SOME CASES EVEN **PERVERT** - - OTHER PEOPLE'S DREAMS.

THE MORE FEAR HE CAUSES, THE MORE POWERFUL HE BECOMES!

SO WHY'S HE WANT YOU AN' PHONEY?

I **BELIEVE** HE WANTS US BOTH FOR THE SAME PURPOSE . . . TO SPEED THE RELEASE OF HIS **MASTER**, THE LORD OF THE LOCUSTS WHO IS TRAPPED IN **STONE**.

THE HOODED ONE THINKS YOUR COUSIN AND I HAVE THE POWER TO HELP FREE HIM.

WHOA, WAIT A MINUTE. I DON'T GET IT . . . **YOU** HAVE A POWER, SO **YOU** MIGHT BE USEFUL, BUT **PHONEY** DOESN'T! WHAT'S SO SPECIAL ABOUT PHONEY?

BESIDES HOW LOUD HE IS!

WELL, DURING THE COW RACE HE TURNED THE TOWNSPEOPLE AGAINST GRAN'MA BEN . . .

THEN HE RILED UP FEAR AND ANGER AT THE **DRAGONS** FOR HIS DRAGONSLAYER SCAM!

THAT'S **EXACTLY** THE KIND OF THING THAT FEEDS THE HOODED ONE'S POWERS.

WE KNOW HE CAUSES TROUBLE, BUT --

BOY, DO WE KNOW!

WE GOT UN OUTTA BONEVILLE BECAUSE PHONEY RAN FOR MAYOR . . .

HEE HEE! {SNORT!} HE CHASED ALL TH' HIGH SOCIETY **MUCKETY-MUCKS** INTO THE **RIVER** WITH A GIANT CAMPAIGN BALLOON OF HIMSELF!

IT'S NOT **FUNNY!**

IT WAS SORTA FUNNY WHEN THE ANGRY MOB ATE A BUNCH OF PHONEY'S ROTTEN **PRUNE TARTS**, AN' HAD TO LEAVE IN A HURRY!

MY **POINT** IS THAT PHONEY WOULD NEVER DO ANYTHING TO HELP THE HOODED ONE **ON PURPOSE!**

I BELIEVE THAT. I DO . . .

BUT WE'RE WALKING INTO A NIGHTMARE AND WE NEED TO BE CAREFUL.

THAT'S WHY THE RAT CREATURES ARE ATTACKING THE VALLEY. EVERY FAMILY THAT IS **TERRORIZED** BRINGS HIM ONE STEP CLOSER TO THE POWER HE NEEDS TO RELEASE HIS **MASTER.**

WHY WOULD **ANYBODY** WANT TO RELEASE THE LORD OF THE LOCUSTS?

BECAUSE ONCE THE LORD OF THE LOCUSTS IS **FREE**, HE HAS TO FIND A HUMAN FORM TO INHABIT.

IF HE TAKES OVER THE **HOODED ONE'S** BODY, THE HOODED ONE WILL BECOME THE MOST POWERFUL BEING IN THE WORLD.

THE LORD OF A NIGHTMARE EARTH.

!

THAT'S IT, THORN. PACK YOUR STUFF. WE'RE GOING TO OLD MAN'S CAVE **RIGHT NOW!** THIS IS **CRAZY** SITTING OUT HERE!

I DON'T TRUST GRAN'MA BEN.

WHY DON'T YOU TRUST HER?! JEEZ, THORN! YOU'RE **FREAKING ME OUT!**

YOU REMEMBER THE STORY GRAN'MA TOLD US ABOUT THE NIGHT MY PARENTS WERE KILLED?

OF COURSE I DO! YOU AND YOUR PARENTS WERE ATTACKED BY **RAT CREATURES.** THE NURSEMAID BETRAYED YOU TO **KINGDOK.**

YES. WE WERE BETRAYED.

I KNOW MANY OF MY CHILDHOOD MEMORIES WERE HIDDEN FROM ME BY GRAN'MA BEN AND THE DRAGONS, BUT A LOT HAVE **RETURNED...**

AND THERE IS ONE THING I'M **SURE** OF--

WE HAD NO NURSEMAID.

SKRIT!

WHO IS THERE?

COME, COME. IT IS NO USE HIDING. I KNOW YOU ARE THERE.

WHO DARES TO TRESSPASS ON **ROQUE JA'S** MOUNTAIN?

. . . HAIL, MASTER OF THE EASTERN BORDER . . .

WELL! ISN'T THIS A SURPRISE! THE HOODED ONE HIMSELF.

WHAT PURPOSE BRINGS THE MIGHTY LEADER OF THE **RAT CREATURE TRIBES** TO VISIT MY HUMBLE DOMAIN?

HUMILITY DOES NOT SUIT YOU, LION . . .

I HAVE TRAVELED FAR TO ASK A **BOON** OF YOU . . .

YOU ASK A FAVOR OF **ME?** **BAH!** YOUR JOURNEY HAS BEEN IN **VAIN**, HOLY ONE --

THE TIME FOR **ALLIANCES** IS PAST. YOUR LACKEY **KINGDOK** SHOULD HAVE DELIVERED **THAT** MESSAGE TO YOU . . .

OR PERHAPS HE DIDN'T HAVE ENOUGH OF HIS **THROAT** LEFT TO **SPEAK** WITH!

YES, I'VE CAPTURED THEM... **TWICE**, IN FACT. WHAT DO YOU WANT THEM FOR?

THAT IS MY CONCERN... BUT TIME IS RUNNING SHORT... ...I MUST HAVE THEM BEFORE THE HARVEST MOON...

CAN YOU **DELIVER** THEM?

THE HARVEST MOON? **BLOOD MOON**, YOU MEAN. WHAT ARE YOU UP TO, STICKEATER?

ARE YOU PLANNING A RITUAL? A **SACRIFICE**, PERHAPS?

ALL MAGIC IS STRONGER WHEN ONE USES THE NATURAL WAXING AND WANING OF THE DREAMING RYTHYMS...

ANSWER ME, ROQUE JA... WILL YOU DO THIS THING FOR ME?

I TRIED TO GIVE THEM TO YOU ONCE **ALREADY**. BUT **KINGDOK** INSISTED I LEAVE THEM WITHOUT PROPER **COMPENSATION**.

I DID END UP WITH HIS **TONGUE**, OF COURSE, BUT I WILL WANT **MORE** NEXT TIME.

YOU WILL BE REWARDED... NAME YOUR PRICE.

JON, **PLEASE** TELL ME GRAN'MA BEN ISN'T QUEEN OF THE VALLEY! **PLEASE---**

I COMMAND YOU TO TAKE A WALK WITH ME.

oh, I'M BEGGIN' YA, MAN...

UM. SORRY.

SHE'S TH' QUEEN.

GAH--- MY LIFE IS GONNA SUCK, ISN'T IT?

NOW, PHONCIBLE, IT'S NOT **THAT** BAD. I'LL TELL YOU WHAT; IF YOU AGREE TO BEHAVE YOURSELF, I PROMISE NOT TO HAVE YOUR HEAD CUT OFF.

ho, ho! THAT'S **RICH**, I'LL SAY.

SO WHAT'S THE **DEAL** WITH ALL THESE MYSTIC WARRIORS? THIS PLACE LOOKS LIKE AN **ARMY CAMP.**

THIS PLACE IS A **SANCTUARY.** IT IS THE CENTER OF ALL THAT IS **TRANSCENDANT** IN THIS WORLD.

YOU DON'T SAY.

DO YOU KNOW, PHONEY, THAT BACK IN THE DAYS OF THE KINGDOM, MY FAMILY USED TO **TRAIN** HERE WITH THE VENI-YAN WARRIORS.

OH, YEAH? TRAIN FOR WHAT?

TO BE IN TWO WORLDS AT ONCE... TO BE **HERE**, IN OUR WORLD, AND AT THE SAME TIME IN THE **DREAMING.**

AND HOW DO YOU DO THAT?

BY CONCENTRATING ON OUR KINSHIP WITH THE REST OF CREATION.

THE DREAMING IS A GREAT RIVER OF POWER THAT FLOWS AROUND US IN ALL DIRECTIONS ...

WHEN WE **DREAM**, WE PEER THROUGH A FOGGY GLASS INTO THE RIVER AND SEE A WORLD THAT IS CONNECTED TO ALL OTHER LIVING THINGS.

THAT DREAMING WORLD EXISTS EVEN WHEN WE ARE AWAKE.

YOU'RE STARTIN' TO SCARE ME, GRAN'MA.

THERE'S MORE TO THE WORLD THAN WHAT YOU SEE WITH YOUR EYES, PHONCIBLE.

PFFF! NOTHIN' **IMPORTANT**.

YOU ARE, WITHOUT A **DOUBT**, THE MOST MATERIALISTIC PERSON I KNOW.

COME. I WANT TO SHOW YOU SOMETHING.

A BUNCH OF PICTURES?

THESE PICTURES TELL A STORY. AND THIS IS THE VERY BEGINING.

BACK WHEN THE **DRAGONS** RULED THE EARTH...

WHEN THE WORLD WAS VERY, VERY NEW, THE **FIRST** DRAGON WAS A QUEEN NAMED **MIM**. MIM MAINTAINED THE DREAMING BY WATCHING ITS FLOW AND KEEPING IT **BALANCED**.

THE **DREAMING** IS A THING OF GREAT DELICACY, AND BALANCE IS MOST IMPORTANT.

MIM WATCHED THE DREAMING WITH **CARE**, AND ALL CREATURES LIVED TOGETHER IN PEACE AND HARMONY...

...UNTIL ONE DAY A SPIRIT KNOWN AS THE **LORD OF THE LOCUSTS** BECAME UNHAPPY.

THE LORD OF THE LOCUSTS WAS A NIGHTMARE BEING WITHOUT **SHAPE** OR **FORM** WHO COULD EXIST ONLY IN THE SPIRIT WORLD.

BUT HE WANTED TO MOVE IN **OUR** WORLD TOO, AND TO DO **THAT** -- TO BECOME PART OF OUR **CRUDE** REALITY -- HE WOULD HAVE TO TAKE POSSESSION OF A **MORTAL BEING'S** FLESH!

HE CHOSE MIM, **QUEEN OF THE DRAGONS**, THE MOST POWERFUL DREAMER IN WORLD.

DRAGONS AREN'T **IMMORTAL**?

DRAGONS LIVE FOR A VERY LONG TIME, BUT THEY ARE MORTAL. EVERYTHING IN **OUR** WORLD IS MORTAL.

THE LORD OF THE LOCUSTS ENTERED HER MIND AND THE QUEEN OF THE DRAGONS WENT **MAD**. BALANCE WAS **LOST**, AND THE WORLD WENT DARK.

TO SAVE THE WORLD, ALL THE OTHER DRAGONS HAD TO MOVE **AGAINST** HER! THEY TURNED HER TO **STONE**, AND THEY **TRAPPED** THE LORD OF THE LOCUSTS INSIDE HER **FOREVER**!

TRAPPED ALIVE?

YES, ALIVE. HE CAN FAINTLY COMMUNICATE WITH BEINGS WHO HAVE UNUSUALLY STRONG DREAMS, BUT TO THIS DAY HE LIES ENCASED IN THE STONE CARCASS OF THE QUEEN OF THE DRAGONS.

AFTER THE FRIGHT CAUSED BY THEIR QUEEN, THE HIGH COUNCIL OF DRAGONS NO LONGER FELT THEY SHOULD BE THE SOLE GUARDIANS OF THE DREAMING...

SO THEY BEGAN TO SEARCH FOR A HUMAN THEY COULD TRUST, AND THEY FOUND A YOUNG GIRL NAMED VEN.

SHE WAS VEN HARVESTAR, THE FIRST QUEEN OF THE HUMANS. SHE WAS MY ANCESTOR, AND THORN'S ANCESTOR.

THESE COINS WERE FORGED BY THE DRAGONS AS A TOKEN OF THE COVENANT BETWEEN OUR TWO RACES TO UPHOLD AND MAINTAIN THE BALANCE OF THE DREAMING, ...

YEAH, YEAH, REAL NICE. LET'S SKIP AHEAD A FEW GENERATIONS. WHAT'S THIS GOT TO DO WITH ME?

A GREAT DEAL.

SOMEONE WANTS TO FREE THE LORD OF THE LOCUSTS ...

WHAT?

... AND THEY NEED YOU TO DO IT.

ME?! WHAT FOR? I DON'T KNOW ANYTHING ABOUT DRAGONS OR EVIL SPIRITS!

THE RAT CREATURES THINK YOU DO.

IT'S A SET-UP! I'M BEING FRAMED!

THE BEST INFORMATION WE HAVE IS THAT THE RAT CREATURES AND A ROGUE VENI-YAN WARRIOR CALLED THE HOODED ONE ARE SEARCHING FOR YOU IN ORDER TO FREE THE ANCIENT LORD OF THE LOCUSTS.

BUT I'M **INNOCENT!** I DON'T KNOW ANYTHING ABOUT THIS! GO GET THE **DRAGON!** YOU HAVE TO STOP THE HOODED ONE!

THE DRAGONS WON'T HELP US. THAT'S WHY I'VE GATHERED THE REMAINING **VENI-YAN** AND REOCCUPIED OLD MAN'S CAVE. IF NEED BE, WE CAN MAKE A LAST STAND HERE.

HIGHNESS--

YOUR **HIGHNESS.** LUCIUS DOWN HAS RETURNED FROM PATROL.

THANK YOU. TELL HIM WHERE TO FIND ME.

LUCIUS! GOOD OL' LUCIUS! **HE'LL** SAVE US! HE WON'T LET **ANYTHING** HAPPEN TO YOU OR THORN! HE'S **CRAZY** ABOUT YA.

YES, LUCIUS HAS ALWAYS BEEN VERY SPECIAL TO MY FAMILY.

WELL, **YOU'LL** SEE! ALL THIS **LOCUST** STUFF IS JUST A SIMPLE MISUNDERSTANDING! WE'LL GET IT ALL STRAIGHTENED OUT, THEN ME AN' MY COUSINS CAN GO **HOME,** AND YOU AN' LUCIUS CAN GET MARRIED, AND THORN CAN--

MARRIED? WHY WOULD LUCIUS AND I GET MARRIED?

BECAUSE YOU GUYS ARE OLD **SWEETHEARTS!** HE **TOLD** ME YOU TWO WERE ALMOST MARRIED ONCE.

THAT'S RIDICULOUS! LUCIUS AND I NEVER EVEN COURTED. WHY, HE WASN'T EVEN **SWEET** ON ME . . .

. . . AT LEAST NOT UNTIL IT WAS TOO LATE.

ROSE!

ANY SIGN OF MY GRANDDAUGHTER, LUCIUS? OR THE MISSING BONE BOYS?

NO, I'M SORRY.

DON'T BE. IF **ANYONE** COULD FIND THEM, IT WOULD BE YOU.

THORN IS USING ALL HER SKILLS TO THROW US OFF HER TRAIL. I'M AFRAID THE DRAGON WAS A GOOD TEACHER.

WHY WOULD THORN **WANT** TO THROW YOU OFF HER TRAIL?

I HAVEN'T EXACTLY GIVEN HER A LOT OF REASONS TO **TRUST** ME.

THERE'S MORE BAD NEWS, ROSIE. THE RAT CREATURES ARE ON THE MOVE AGAIN. THE **HOODED ONE** IS SETTING UP ENCAMPMENTS ON ALL SIDES OF US.

HOLY SMOKES!

FONE BONE'S OUT THERE!

THERE'S STILL TIME TO KEEP A PATH CLEAR TO THE SOUTH IF WE SEND A UNIT TONIGHT.

WELL GO! GO! WHAT'RE YA **WAITIN'** ON, YA BIG APE?! FONE BONE AN' SMILEY ARE **OUT** THERE!

LET HIM BE, LUCIUS. HE'S JUST WORRIED ABOUT HIS COUSINS.

RRRR... IF YOU SAY SO.

YOU'RE LUCKY SOMEBODY'S LOOKIN' **OUT** FOR YOU, RUNT. OTHERWISE I'D TWIST YER SCRAWNY **NECK!**

YEAH, YEAH. I HEAR THAT A LOT LATELY.

WHO **IS** THIS HOODED ONE ANYWAY?

I WISH I KNEW.

OKAY, OKAY, JUST FOR THE SAKE OF **ARGUMENT**, SUPPOSE ALL THIS DREAM STUFF IS **REAL**...

...WHAT WOULD **ACTUALLY HAPPEN** IF THE HOODED ONE MANAGED TO SET THE **LORD OF THE LOCUSTS** FREE?

WHY, THE END OF THE WORLD, OF COURSE.

YOU ARE SO WEIRD.

CHIN UP, PHONCIBLE. WE WON'T GIVE UP THE VALLEY WITHOUT A FIGHT.

NOW IF YOU'LL EXCUSE ME, I'D BETTER GO CHECK OUR PROVISIONS.

NEXT: THE SIEGE

HEY!! WATCH WHAT **YOU'RE DOING!** THAT'S MY **BATHWATER** YOU'RE SPILLIN'!

SINCE WHEN DO YOU LIKE TO **BATHE?** YOU'RE USUALLY LIKE A **CAT** WHEN IT COMES TO GETTING WET.

SINCE WE'VE BEEN LIVING IN THE MOUNTAINS FOR **WEEKS!** A GENTLEMAN CAN ONLY TAKE SO MUCH **CAKED-ON DIRT.**

SAY -- DO YOU HEAR THAT?

WHAT IS THAT?

SOUNDS LIKE A WOLF.

OH! BUT IT'S NOT A RAT CREATURE, THOUGH, RIGHT?

NO, IT'S JUST SOME LONELY OLD WOLF CALLING OUT INTO THE TWILIGHT.

SOUNDS KINDA SAD, DOESN'T IT?

YOU THINK HE'LL COME HERE?

THE WOLF? IF HE DOES, TED WILL TURN HIM AWAY.

C'MON, LET'S GET THIS WATER AROUND BACK.

Y'KNOW, FONE BONE, IT FEELS **GOOD** TO BE BACK AT GRAN'MA BEN'S FARMHOUSE. IT'S ALMOST LIKE BEING HOME AGAIN.

HAS THORN SAID WHAT THE **PLAN** IS? WE'RE NOT LEAVING RIGHT AWAY, ARE WE?

THAT'S THORN'S DECISION.

WELL, WHAT DOES SHE **WANT**? ARE WE GONNA STAY HERE, OR ARE WE GONNA GO TO OLD MAN'S CAVE?

NEITHER.

SHE JUST WANTS TO GET SOME THINGS AND GO BACK TO THE MOUNTAINS.

IT'S GRAN'MA BEN, ISN'T IT? THORN DOESN'T TRUST HER ANYMORE.

NOPE. SHE DOESN'T TRUST HER.

WELL, I THINK THORN'S **WRONG**. I THINK WE **CAN** TRUST GRAN'MA BEN, AND WE SHOULD GO MEET HER AT OLD MAN'S CAVE, LIKE TED WANTS US TO!

SO DO I . . .

... BUT UNTIL THORN CHANGES HER MIND, WE'LL JUST HAVE TO BE PATIENT.

AT LEAST UNTIL WE HEAR THIS BIG **PLAN** OF HERS.

YOU THINK SHE REALLY **HAS** A PLAN?

I SURE HOPE SO. A PLAN TO SAVE US FROM THE RAT CREATURES, **AND** TO DEAL WITH THEIR LEADER **THE HOODED ONE.**

HMMF.

IF THORN **DID** HAVE A PLAN, WHY WOULDN'T SHE TELL IT TO US?

THE PLAN IS TO SNEAK INTO THE RAT CREATURES' ENCAMPMENT AND **ASSASSINATE** THE HOODED ONE . . .

THE REASON I HAVEN'T TOLD YOU ABOUT IT IS BECAUSE I'M GOING ALONE.

I'VE MADE ARRANGEMENTS WITH TED FOR THE BOTH OF YOU TO STAY HERE AT THE FARMHOUSE.

TED WILL HELP YOU FIND FOOD. YOU'LL BE SAFER HERE THAN YOU WOULD BE AT OLD MAN'S CAVE.

NOW WAIT -- WHOA, WHOA.

WHAT ARE YOU TALKING ABOUT?

YOU THINK AFTER ALL THIS, WE'RE NOT GOING TO BE PART OF THE PLAN?

ALTHOUGH I FEEL I SHOULD **STRESS** THAT IT IS A VERY **STUPID** PLAN.

THIS DOESN'T INVOLVE YOU.

IT'S MY PROBLEM.

DOESN'T INVOLVE ME?! THE HOODED ONE IS AFTER **MY COUSIN PHONEY BONE!** "THE ONE WHO BEARS THE STAR," **REMEMBER?**

NOT TO MENTION THAT I'VE BEEN CHASED OFF CLIFFS, PUSHED OFF WATERFALLS, **RAINED ON**, AND BEATEN UP EVERY SINGLE DAY SINCE I **GOT** TO THIS STUPID VALLEY!

WE'RE **IN**, THORN --

YOU'RE NOT MAKING THIS DECISION **WITHOUT** US!

AND BEFORE YOU SAY ANOTHER WORD -- I KNOW YOU'RE MAD AT YOUR GRANDMOTHER FOR LYING ABOUT THE DEATH OF YOUR PARENTS, BUT **MOVE ON.**

SHE THOUGHT SHE WAS PROTECTING YOU.

C'MON, THORN.

LET'S GO TO OLD MAN'S CAVE.

IT'S NOT JUST HER LIES. THERE'S MORE . . .

ALMOST EVERY NIGHT GRAN'MA BEN APPEARS TO ME IN A DREAM . . .

BUT SOMETHING IS WRONG.

SHE SEEMS SPLIT IN TWO . . .

FIRST PULLING ME IN ONE DIRECTION, THEN ANOTHER. IT'S LIKE HAVING TWO DIFFERENT GRAN'MA BENS BATTLING FOR POSSESSION OF ME.

IT'S JUST A DREAM --

IT'S **NOT** JUST A DREAM! YOU DON'T KNOW WHAT IT'S LIKE.

YOU DON'T KNOW WHAT IT'S LIKE TO NEVER KNOW YOUR MOTHER AND FATHER.

YES, WE DO.

WHAT DID YOU SAY?

WE'RE ORPHANS, TOO. ME, AND FONE BONE, AND PHONEY. WE'RE ALL THE FAMILY WE **GOT.**

UNTIL WE CAME HERE, THAT IS. YOU AND GRAN'MA BEN TOOK CARE OF US -- EVEN WHEN IT MEANT YOUR OWN LIVES WOULD BE IN DANGER.

WHEN WE WERE KIDS, PHONEY WAS THE OLDEST AND HE TOOK CARE OF US.

I ALWAYS FIGURED THAT WAS **WHY** HE GOT SO RESOURCEFUL AND STINGY.

WHEN PHONEY PULLS SOME STUPID SCAM THAT MAKES ME **CRAZY**, I KNOW DEEP DOWN HE DOESN'T MEAN TO HURT ANYONE . . . . . . IN **HIS** MIND, HE'S STILL LOOKING OUT FOR US.

DEEP DOWN YOU KNOW IF YOU CAN TRUST SOMEONE.

ALL RIGHT, FONE BONE. ALL RIGHT , SMILEY BONE. WE'LL GO TO OLD MAN'S CAVE.

I GUESS . . . DEEP DOWN, I **DO** TRUST GRAN'MA BEN.

GRAB YOUR STUFF, AND LET'S GO.

MAN, I HOPE YOU'RE RIGHT ABOUT THIS!

HEY, **THORN!** CAN I WEAR SOME OF THAT WAR PAINT, TOO? HUH, CAN I?

HOLD UP.

THIS IS *GOOD* -- WE SPLIT UP HERE.

WENDELL, HAVE YOUR MEN DIG IN. REMEMBER, YOU ARE OUR LAST LINE OF DEFENSE --

WE **MUST NOT** LET THE RAT CREATURES CROSS THIS RIVER. IF WE DO, OLD MAN'S CAVE WILL BE SURROUNDED.

CAPTAIN KNOTT, MOVE YOUR MEN FORWARD IN A LINE AND HOLD. WAIT FOR THE SIGNAL.

YES, SIR.

SCOUTS FOLLOW ME.

WHAT TH--?

DO YOU NOT RECOGNIZE ME? HAS IT BEEN SO LONG?

B-- BRIAR?

IS IT REALLY YOU--?

YES, LUCIUS... IT IS REALLY ME. COME CLOSER...

YOU CAN NOT KNOW HOW PAINFUL IT HAS BEEN TO BE APART FROM YOU... I HAVE ACHED TO BE WITH YOU...

TELL ME... HOW IS MY BABY SISTER...? HOW IS ROSE? HAVE YOU TAKEN GOOD CARE OF HER?

YOUR MAJESTY . . .

STILL NO WORD FROM LUCIUS DOWN.

WE'VE SENT OUT A TEAM OF WARRIORS TO RE-ESTABLISH CONTACT.

MOST OF THE VILLAGERS ARE SAFELY IN THE CAVE.

AND STILL NO SIGN OF THORN?

I THOUGHT NOT.

PLEASE KEEP THE CAMP ON ALERT, CAPTAIN.

NOW WHERE WERE WE, PHONCIBLE?

YOU WERE TALKING ABOUT MY SOUL.

AH, YES, YOUR SOUL IS THAT BIT OF THE DREAMING THAT MAKES YOU YOU.

YEAH, YEAH. EVERYTHING'S A BIG DREAM TO YOU, ISN'T IT, ROSE?

EACH OF US, IN FACT, IS A SMALL CONCENTRATED BIT OF DREAM CARRIED ALONG IN THE CURRENTS OF THE GREAT DREAMING RIVER THAT FLOWS ALL AROUND US.

WITHIN OURSELVES... THE DREAMING MAY FLOW IN MANY DIRECTIONS. BUT OCCASIONALLY THERE IS ONE BORN WITHIN WHOM ALL THE CURRENTS ARE ALIGNED.

SUCH A PERSON WOULD BE VERY **STRONG** AND GIFTED BY FATE.

THORN IS SUCH A PERSON. PERHAPS YOU ARE TOO.

HMM, WELL. STRONG AND GIFTED... THAT **IS** HARD TO DENY, BUT I STILL DON'T SEE WHY THE HOODED ONE WANTS MY SOUL --

oh...

GRAN'MA? WHAT'S WRONG?

IT -- IT'S THE **GITCHY FEELIN'**... THAT **TERRIBLE** FEELING THAT MAKES YOUR HEAD SWIM AND YOUR LEGS WOBBLE! IT'S A POWERFUL **OMEN** OF BAD THINGS TO COME!

ARE YOU GONNA BE OKAY?

HOLY SMOKE. DID HE GET LOOSE?!

NO. BUT HE'S STIRRING.

HMM. BLOOD MOON. THAT'S A BAD SIGN.

YOUR HIGHNESS! LUCIUS IS OUTSIDE THE CAMP! HE AND HIS MEN ARE BEING PURSUED BY RAT CREATURES!

GET THEM INSIDE AND SECURE THE GATES.

LUCIUS! WHAT HAPPENED?

THE RATS CAUGHT US BY THE RIVER AND SLAUGHTERED US. IF REINFORCEMENTS HADN'T ARRIVED, WE WOULD'VE BEEN FINISHED.

I SHOULD HAVE BEEN WITH YOU.

I WISH YOU HAD BEEN . . . HERE. TAKE HIM. I DON'T KNOW IF HE'S STILL ALIVE OR NOT.

IT'S ALL MY FAULT, ROSE. THE RAT CREATURES HAVE US COMPLETELY SURROUNDED.

CALM. BE CALM. WE MUST PREPARE FOR OUR FINAL STAND.

I JUST PRAY THAT THORN IS SAFE . . . WHEREVER SHE IS.

NEXT: HARVEST MOON

I'M SORRY, ROSE.

IT MUST BE THE LORD OF THE LOCUSTS. HE'S KEPT HER ALIVE ALL THESE YEARS...

...AND NOW SHE IS GOING TO REPAY THAT DEBT BY SETTING HIM FREE.

WE CAN'T WIN THIS ALONE.

IF EVER WE NEEDED THE GREAT RED DRAGON, WE NEED HIM NOW.

I KNOW... BUT THE COUNCIL'S DECISION WAS FINAL

ROSE!

THERE'S NOTHING WE CAN DO TO CHANGE THEIR MINDS?

I PLEADED WITH THE HIGH COUNCIL IN DEREN GARD FOR THREE DAYS... EVEN WITH THE RED DRAGON BY MY **SIDE** I WAS UNABLE TO SWAY THEM.

...THE DRAGONS ARE GOING UNDERGROUND FOR GOOD.

WE FACE THE END ALONE.

ROSE!

IT'S ALL RIGHT, CAPTAIN. WHAT IS IT, WENDELL?

GIVE HIM TO US, ROSE!

YEAH! THIS IS ALL HIS FAULT!

WHOSE FAULT, DEAR?

PHONEY BONE! "THE ONE WHO BEARS THE STAR!"

HE'S THE ONE THE RAT CREATURES ARE AFTER. THEY TORE UP THE VALLEY LOOKING FOR HIM.

YEAH! NOW THE RAT CREATURES HAVE US SURROUNDED! IF HE'S ALL THEY WANT, LET'S HAND HIM OVER!

EVEN IF HE WAS ALL THE RAT CREATURES WANTED, I WOULDN'T ADVISE GIVING THEM THE ONE THING THEY NEED TO WIN THIS WAR.

WHAT DO YOU MEAN?

OUR FRIENDS OUT THERE BELIEVE THAT THE "ONE WHO BEARS THE STAR" CAN FREE THE ANCIENT LORD OF THE LOCUSTS.

LORD OF TH --?

YOU MEAN THAT OLD FABLE ABOUT THE QUEEN OF THE DRAGONS?

OH, FER--

--THAT'S JUST A STORY! GIVE THEM PHONEY BONE AND LET 'EM TRY! WHAT CAN THE LORD OF THE LOCUSTS DO TO US?

THE LORD OF THE LOCUSTS CAN STEAL THE DREAMING THAT FLOWS THROUGH YOU.

WHY DON'T YOU TAKE THAT **STICK-EATER** MUMBO JUMBO BACK TO THE **WOODS**, YOU --

BACK OFF, WENDELL. THE ENEMY'S **OUTSIDE** THE GATES, REMEMBER?

HEY -- WHERE'S PHONEY? TH' LITTLE RAT IS **GONE!**

HE LEFT THIS.

IT'S HIS SHIRT.

SON OF A --

HE'S ESCAPED!

HE RAN AWAY BECAUSE YOU SCARED HIM! QUICKLY! WE HAVE TO FIND HIM!

SPREAD OUT AND SEARCH THE CAMP -- **FIND THAT BONE!** IF HE ENDS UP IN THE WRONG HANDS, IT'S GOING TO BE A REAL SHORT WAR.

HOLD IT RIGHT THERE, SQUIRT!

GRAN'MA --

WHERE DO YOU THINK YOU'RE GOING?

I HAD TO RUN AWAY...

HAVEN'T YOU CAUSED ENOUGH TROUBLE?

EVERYONE WAS IN DANGER AS LONG AS I STAYED THERE...

...I'M THE ONE THE RAT CREATURES WANT.

I THOUGHT IF I LEFT, THE REST OF YOU WOULD BE SAFE!

HORSE KNOBBIES!! YOU DON'T CARE ABOUT ANYBODY'S SAFETY! YOU WERE RUNNING AWAY...

BAM! oof!

FONE BONE!

PHONEY! WHAT ARE YOU DOING HERE?

AND WHY ARE YOU NAKED?

YOU GUYS GOTTA GET AWAY FROM ME! EVERYBODY'S AFTER ME BECAUSE I WEAR A STAR ON MY SHIRT!

COME WITH US, PHONEY, WE'RE GOING TO OLD MAN'S CAVE. YOU'LL BE SAFE THERE.

NO! I JUST LEFT THERE! THE RAT CREATURES HAVE THE PLACE SURROUNDED.

SURROUNDED?

WHERE'S GRAN'MA BEN?

BACK THERE! A GIANT LION ATTACKED HER--

JUST NOW? WHY DIDN'T YOU SAY SO?

DON'T, THORN! YOU'LL BE KILLED!

WAIT, THORN! YOU CAN'T FIGHT THAT LION -- LET'S FIND THE **DRAGON!**

FORGET IT--

THE DRAGONS WON'T HELP US -- GRAN'MA SAID THEY'VE GONE UNDERGROUND FOR GOOD.

BUT --

HEY! HEY!

IT'S **ROCKJAW!**

WELL!

PRINCESS THORN, I PRESUME . . .

ROCK JAW!

LOOK OUT, THORN!

KRAK!

STAND ASIDE, BONE! I NEED THE BODY.

GET AWAY!!

uuuuhh....

WAKE UP,
FONE BONE.

THORN!
LOOK OUT!

WAKE UP
NOW.

DRAGON! THORN WAS ATTACKED BY
ROCK JAW! I THINK
SHE MIGHT BE HURT!

SHE WAS HURT VERY BADLY.

IS SHE - - ?
I MEAN IS SHE - - ?

SHE IS ALIVE...

...BUT JUST BARELY.
YOU MUST HURRY
OR SHE WILL
DIE.

...ROSE...
GO AFTER THEM.

DON'T TALK, LUCIUS. SAVE YOUR STRENGTH.

THERE. THAT SHOULD STOP THE BLEEDING.

GOOD. THAT'S ALL YOU CAN DO. NOW **GO AFTER THAT LION!**

NO. I HAVE TO GET YOU BACK TO THE CAVE.

ROSE -- STOP.

I'LL GET MYSELF BACK. YOU HAVE TO BEAT THAT LION TO PHONEY BONE-- OR **WORSE**... YOU HAVE TO BEAT HIM TO **THORN**.

I CAN WALK, SEE?

ALL RIGHT, LUCIUS.
GOODBYE.

GOODBYE, ROSE.

YOU CHASED ME ALL OVER KINGDOM COME BECAUSE OF *THAT?!*

O BOY.

FONE BONE IS GONNA BE CRANKY WHEN HE FINDS OUT ABOUT THIS.

IT'S PHONEY'S **CAMPAIGN BALLOON!** THE ONE THAT CHASED **MISS CRAB-BONE** INTO THE RIVER!

YEAH! THE SAME BALLOON THAT GOT US RUN OUT OF BONEVILLE IN THE FIRST PLACE.

I THOUGHT YOU CAUGHT IT AND LET THE AIR OUT OF IT!

I THOUGHT *YOU* DID! IT MUST HAVE FLOATED HERE ACROSS THE DESERT.

AS SOON AS WE SAVE HIM FROM THIS SACRIFICE, LET'S **KILL** HIM!

THIS IS WHY YOU'VE BEEN SEARCHING FOR ME?! IT'S A CAMPAIGN BALLOON! THE BANNER USED TO SAY: PHONCIBLE P. BONE WILL GET YOUR **VOTE!**

I WILL NOW USE MY SCYTHE . . . TO CONNECT YOUR **SOUL** . . . DIRECTLY TO THE LIVING ROCK . . .

BRIAR!

THAT BONE CREATURE IS NOT THE VENI-YAN-CARI. LET HIM GO!

AH, **WELCOME**, ROSE HARVESTAR . . . MY **SISTER** . . . .

WHERE IS SHE, BRIAR?

I CONFESS, MY SISTER... THAT SEEING YOU ALIVE IS QUITE AMAZING...

....I HAD THOUGHT YOU DIED THE SAME NIGHT I DID.

WHERE IS SHE, BRIAR?

HERE... IS YOUR PRECIOUS VENI-YAN-CARI...

THE ONE YOU THOUGHT WOULD BE THE FUTURE RULER OF THE LAND...

...BUT SHE IS DEAD!

AS YOU BOTH SHOULD HAVE BEEN FIFTEEN YEARS AGO ON THAT MOUNTAIN PASS...

WHAT YOU HAVE KILLED, BRIAR, IS YOUR ONLY CHANCE TO FREE YOUR MASTER -- THE LORD OF THE LOCUSTS.

EVEN I CAN SEE THIS BALLOON IS NO OMEN OF POWER -- IT IS MERELY A SYMBOL OF PRIDE AND VANITY!

YOUR JEALOUSY OF THE TRUE VENI-YAN-CARI HAS BLINDED YOU -- AND YOU HAVE BADLY MISCALCULATED, MY SISTER.

NO . . .

NO, I HAVE NOT MISCALCULATED... HE **HAS** THE POWER TO FREE OUR MASTER -- HE **MUST!**

LISTEN, SIS . . . I ENJOY A HOSTILE TAKEOVER AS MUCH AS THE NEXT GUY, BUT FACE **FACTS!** YOU BLEW IT!

RRRRR!

RRRURLL....

WHAT HAVE YOU **DONE**, STICK-EATER?

IT WAS THE **PRINCESS** WE NEEDED, NOT THE BONE! AND YOU HAD HER **KILLED!**

YOU HAVE BROUGHT DISGRACE UPON OUR PEOPLE IN THE EYES OF THE LORD OF THE LOCUSTS . . .

WAIT --

DID YOU FEEL THAT?

SOMETHING MOVED DEEP IN THE EARTH!

FONE BONE! NO!

I'M GOING DOWN THERE!

THOOM

THOOM! hisss

NEXT: ENDGAME